GALE

CENGAGE Learning

Drama for Students, Volume 3

Staff

Editorial: David M. Galens, *Editor*. Terry Browne, Christopher Busiel, Clare Cross, Tom Faulkner, John Fiero, David M. Galens, Carole Hamilton, Sheri Metzger, Daniel Moran, Terry Nienhuis, William P. Wiles, Joanne Woolway, Etta Worthington, *Entry Writers*. Elizabeth Cranston, Kathleen J. Edgar, Jennifer Gariepy, Dwayne D. Hayes, Kurt Kuban, Joshua Kondek, Tom Ligotti, Scot Peacock, Patti Tippett, Pam Zuber, *Contributing Editors*. James Draper, *Managing Editor*. Diane Telgen, *"For Students" Line Coordinator*. Jeffery Chapman, *Programmer/Analyst*.

Research: Victoria B. Cariappa, *Research Team Manager*. Andy Malonis, Barb McNeil, *Research Specialists*. Julia C. Daniel, Tamara C. Nott, Tracie A. Richardson, Cheryl L. Warnock, *Research Associates*. Phyllis P. Blackman, Jeffrey D. Daniels,

Corrine A. Stocker, *Research Assistants*.

Permissions: Susan M. Trosky, *Permissions Manager*. Kimberly F. Smilay, *Permissions Specialist*. Steve Cusack and Kelly A. Quin, *Permissions Associates*.

Production: Mary Beth Trimper, *Production Director*. Evi Seoud, *Assistant Production Manager*. Shanna Heilveil, *Production Assistant*.

Graphic Services: Randy Bassett, *Image Database Supervisor*. Robert Duncan and Michael Logusz, *Imaging Specialists*. Pamela A. Reed, *Photography Coordinator*. Gary Leach, *Macintosh Artist*.

Product Design: Cynthia Baldwin, *Product Design Manager*. Cover Design: Michelle DiMercurio, *Art Director*. Page Design: Pamela A. E. Galbreath, *Senior Art Director*.

editors or publisher. Errors brought to the attention of the publisher and verified to the satisfaction of the publisher will be corrected in future editions.

This publication is a creative work fully protected by all applicable copyright laws, as well as by misappropriation, trade secret, unfair competition, and other applicable laws. The authors and editors of this work have added value to the underlying factual material herein through one or more of the following: unique and original selection, coordination, expression, arrangement, and classification of information. All rights to this publication will be vigorously defended.

Copyright © 1998
Gale Research
835 Penobscot Building
645 Griswold
Detroit, MI 48226-4094

This book is printed on acid-free paper that meets the minimum requirements of American National Standard for Information Sciences—Permanence Paper for Printed Library Materials, ANSI Z39.48-1984.

ISBN 0-7876-2752-6
ISSN 1094-9232
Printed in the United States of America

10 9 8 7 6 5 4 3 2

Marat/Sade

Peter Weiss

1964

Introduction

Whether reading or watching a performance, *Marat/ Sade* is neither a comfortable nor an immediately enjoyable play. The work, whose full title is *The Persecution and Assassination of Jean-Paul Marat As Performed by the Inmates of the Asylum of Charenton under the Direction of The Marquis de Sade*, is more commonly known by its truncated name. The play was first performed in West Berlin at the Schiller Theater in 1964 and directed by

Konrad Swinarksi. It was not until British director Peter Brook staged an English language version in London, however, that Weiss and his play received wide acclaim. That production, staged in 1964 at the Aldwych Theatre, brought *Marat/Sade* to the attention of the world as critics and audiences hailed the play's unique style and structure.

Swinarksi's direction was tame compared to what Brook would do to the work in London and, the following year, in New York. According to David Richard Jones in *Great Directors at Work: Stanislavsky, Brecht, Kazan, Brook:* "Most audiences experienced it as powerful. Viewers showed that they were strongly affected by its magnitude, whether they walked out in anger or stayed seated, shaking, at the end. The show usually had a similar impact on critics, other theatre workers, and the actors themselves."

Audience members did storm out of performances of *Marat/Sade;* some viewers reacted so strongly that they became ill. "At least one spectator, the German actress Ruth Arrack, died in the auditorium during a performance," reported Jones. The fever pitch of the play's emotions, combined with its frank violence and brutality, led many of the play's detractors to label it as nothing more than "shock theatre."

Debate existed among critics about the value of the play. Some suggested that the real meaning of the play was perhaps ambiguous. The majority of critics, however, felt that the ambiguity of the play was intentional and a means to force the audience to assess the proceedings and come to their own conclusions. Despite what some perceived as a lack of resolution in *Marat/Sade*, all who viewed the production agreed that it was a spectacle the likes of which the London and New York stages rarely saw.

Peter Ulrich Weiss was born on November 8, 1916, in Nowawes, a German province near Berlin. A textile merchant, his father was a Hungarian of Jewish descent. His mother, a German Christian, was a former actress. At three, he and his family moved to Bremen, which is the city Weiss associates with childhood and his first rebellion against the wealth and the social pressures of an upper middle class upbringing. In his adolescence the family moved to Berlin, where Weiss began training for a career as a visual artist. His life changed drastically, however, when Adolf Hitler's National Socialist Party (the Nazis) rose to political power in Germany. The Nazis were racial purists who believed that non-Germans were a detriment to society and should be rooted out. Being half Jewish and a Czech citizen Weiss was a particular target for such oppression.

As the Nazi's persecution of Jews became more violent, the Weiss family fled Germany in 1935, settling near London where Weiss was sent to take photography classes, since his family felt that painters couldn't make a decent living. In his spare time, however, he continued to paint, using his attic as a studio. His disavowal of his family's values (and wealth) forced him out on his own, and he pursued his studies as an artist in London. He later studied at the Art Academy in Prague, Czechoslovakia, and struck up a friendship with author Herman Hesse (*Siddartha*), whose work he had been reading for years. Although painting was his major passion, Weiss began writing as well. In 1939, his family moved to Sweden, and Weiss went along, later joining a commune of other German-speaking artists in Sweden.

During this period, Weiss began writing more seriously, publishing his first book in Swedish in 1944. Returning to Germany as a journalist following World War II, he started writing in dramatic form and produced a radio play, *The Tower*, in 1948. Gradually, the majority of his creative work focused on writing, although he also made documentary and feature films. His fiction work included two autobiographical novels, *The Leavetaking* and *Vanishing Point*.

The 1964 production of his play *Marat/Sade* established Weiss as a writer of international acclaim. The play, with its daring style and strong political content, won a number of honors, including a Lessing Preis Award, an Antionette ("Tony") Perry Award, and the Drama Critics' Circle Award for best play. The drama was produced in London and New York with direction by Peter Brooks, who many credit as much as Weiss with defining the work's unique structure.

Like *Marat/Sade*, later plays by Weiss continued a political vein, these works include *Trotsky in Exile, Vietnam Discourse*, and *The Investigation*, which is about Nazi War Crime trials.

Weiss died in Sweden in 1982 and was

posthumously awarded the Georg Buchner Prize for outstanding achievement in German letters. Although some critics have considered his work too heavy in political agenda, Roger Ellis said in *Peter Weiss in Exile: A Critical Study of His Works:* "Weiss always sought something contemporary in his studies of the past: an understanding of the roots of social violence, of the extent of human influence upon historical development, of the restrictive conditions which bear upon modern artists and how to overcome them, and, most especially, an understanding of the roots of the seemingly paradoxical faith of certain individuals who struggle unsuccessfully to improve apparently hopeless situations."

Or, in Weiss's own words, "I myself think that art should be so strong that it changes life; otherwise it is a failure."

Plot Summary

Act I

Marat/Sade is set in the bath hall of an insane asylum at Charenton; the time is some years after the French Revolution. The play opens with the Marquis de Sade undertaking some last minute preparations for a play he has written with the parts to be played by inmates of the asylum. Invited to watch this spectacle are members of the French aristocracy, specifically Coulmier, the director of the clinic, and his family. Sade gives a signal and Coulmier and his family enter as the actors, a scraggly lot of patients from the asylum, wait tensely.

Coulmier introduces this play within a play by describing the modern advanced treatment at Charenton, which includes therapy through education and art. The Herald points out the main characters—Sade who is seated in his dais, Jean-Paul Marat who is placed in his bath, and Charlotte Corday. There is also Duperret, who buzzes around Corday trying to get his hands on her, and the radical priest Jacques Roux. The Herald explains each of the characters as well as the story line. Corday is coming to Paris to murder Marat in his bath.

At this point the cast pauses to offer an homage to Marat and engage in a slight discussion of his role. This sequence ends with a refrain that will be repeated throughout the play:

> *Marat, we're poor and the poor stay poor/Marat don't make us wait any more/We want our rights and we don't care how/We want our revolution NOW*

Emotions rise as this is recited and the patients/actors become agitated; the asylum's nurses restrain them. Coulmier complains to Sade about this outburst, calling on him to control what is happening on stage.

At this point Corday is introduced and her role in the play explained further. Marat, cared for by his mistress Simonne in his bathtub, claims, "I am the Revolution." Corday makes her first attempt to contact him, knocking at his door. She is sent away, reminded by Simonne that she must come three times before gaining entrance. The Four Singers then describe Corday's visit to Paris and she responds. Marat, in his bath, attacks the conduct of the ruling class after the revolution, and the patients mime an execution. They play with the severed head, kicking and throwing it about the stage. Coulmier breaks into this play in progress, suggesting that this violence isn't helping the patients. The Herald smooths things over by declaring that of course this play is talking about the past. Then Sade and Marat launch into a conversation about life and death, in which Sade ultimately looks at war and the manner in which anonymous deaths are parceled out. He wonders whether Marat has become an aristocrat because he has questioned Sade's lack of compassion.

Marat makes an indictment against the status quo, including the way the church has been used to keep the poor in place by encouraging them to view suffering as an honor. This statement is too much for Coulmier, who again questions Sade about the cuts in the play that they had supposedly agreed upon. Sade and Marat continue to talk, Sade suggesting that his health may be the most important thing to Marat, who then lashes out at the ruling class, complaining of how oppressed people still are.

Duperret is introduced and talks with Corday about her plans, but he (or the patient playing him) is more interested in touching her body and must have his attention refocused. Sade taunts Marat, questioning the validity of the revolution, pointing out that everything comes down to the personal, to oneself. Roux speaks up and encourages a continued revolution of the masses but is restrained. This is too much for Coulmier and he again protests the events taking place in Sade's play. Roux appeals to Marat and Coulmier demands the scene be cut. Sade continues his conversation with Marat and talks of confronting the criminal in himself while he has Corday beat him. Marat sits in his bath and asks for his pen and paper so he can write down his ideas. He wonders aloud if the revolution that has taken place has improved things. Sade questions Marat's ideology.

Corday makes a second attempt to see Marat

and is turned away. Sade taunts Marat about the reasons people join the revolution. Marat is visited by voices from his past and feverishly begs for help in writing down his thoughts. The act ends with the repeated demand from the patient/actors for revolution.

Act II

The second act opens with an imagined scene in the National Assembly where Marat questions the actions of those in power after the revolution, saying they are as bad as before the revolution. His words are received with mixed emotions. Some cheer him on while others question his facts and intentions, including Duperret. Coulmier can take it no longer and jumps up, demanding Sade cut these parts from the play. Roux interrupts and further incites the patients.

Marat, exhausted, is in his bath again, tended to by Simonne. He is once again attempting to commit his thoughts to paper. Sade, to the side, questions the revolutionary's writing, claiming that nothing can be achieved by scribbling. Marat defends himself, saying that he always wrote with action in mind and that it wasn't a replacement for action, only a preparation. But Sade doesn't let up and asks him to look at the sorry state of the revolution. Marat is confused and exhausted.

Corday prepares herself for her final visit to Marat's bath. She takes her dagger in hand, while Duperret suggests she throw it away and give up on this goal. He begs her to go away with him. She refuses and resolutely goes to Marat's door. Sade interjects his idea about sensuality at this point and stirs up the patients to sing "what's the point of a revolution without general copulation." Corday knocks at Marat's door and is invited to enter.

The Herald engages in a brief recitation of history, claiming fifteen glorious years since the revolution and the rise of Napoleon. Marat is killed in his bath by Corday.

Coulmier tries to bring a conclusion, again insisting "we live in far different times." The patients, however, are aroused and march around the stage. Coulmier enlists the nurses to strike them down. As the nurses violently beat the patients, Sade looks on laughing. The play ends.

Characters

Charlotte Corday

Corday exists in a dream and must at times be ushered to her appointed times and places. She speaks in a sing-song voice, never fully dimensional, but resolute even in her dream-like state. It is not explained whether her behavior is historical or merely the personality traits of the mental patient playing her in Sade's inner play. Like other characters in the play within the play, Corday's ambiguous nature inspires disturbing feelings in the audience.

Corday is going to murder Marat. She comes to Paris, buys the knife, and confers with Duperret, who, at the last minute, tries to dissuade her from committing the murder. She is determined, however, to accomplish this mission. She also interacts with Sade, and in what many consider a startling scene in Brook's production, lashes Sade at his request—not with a whip but with her hair.

Corday approaches the thought of killing Marat with fascination. The manner in which she describes how she will kill him is spiked with eroticism. She views Marat's murder as an act that will free humankind. She once found Marat's ideas appealing, but she is disappointed by the revolution's outcome. She sees his death as the first step in a new revolution. Near the end, Corday envisions her own death at the guillotine.

Media Adaptations

- A filmed version of Brook's staging of *Marat/ Sade* was produced in 1966. The original cast is featured, including Glenda Jackson as Corday. Video is available from Waterbearer Films, Lumivision, and I.S. Productions.

- Caedmon produced a sound recording in 1967 called *Peter Weiss Reading from His Works*. This includes several scenes from *Marat/Sade*.

- An audio recording of the Brook production of *Marat/Sade* was issued by Caedmon and includes original cast members from the early

productions   by   the   Royal
Shakespeare   Company.   Available
from Caedmon.

Coulmier

Coulmier is the director of the mental asylum, quite smug about the advanced treatment employed by the Charenton asylum; he boasts of the progress they have made using art and music in therapy. He interrupts Sade's play on several occasions, complaining about inciteful sections that should be removed. He also interjects to assure anyone listening that the disgraceful subjects in Sade's play occurred long ago and that things are much better now. His nervousness increases as the patients are aroused and, in the final scene, he orders the nurses to brutally beat down the rioting patients.

Duperret

Duperret is a rather foppish character whose mind is constantly on sex. He takes any opportunity he can to manhandle women, whether it is Corday, who ignores his advances, or the wife and daughter of Coulmier, who at first don't know how to react to him and later merely push him away. He coaxes Corday along on her mission but tries to talk her out of the murder just before she commits it. He entreats her to leave Paris with him.

Like all of the characters in Sade's inner play,

Duperret is essayed by an insane actor. His actions are never defined as those of a sane participant in Marat's murder or those of a psychotic patient. His relentless and overt sexual behavior seems to indicate that the personality of the patient is spilling over into the character, however.

Simonne Evrard

She is the mistress of Marat and regularly fusses over him and changes his bandages. She sends Corday away twice but on the assassin's third visit, Simonne allows her to enter.

Four Singers

Like the Herald, these four report what is happening throughout the play, through music and mime. They are partly comic.

Herald

The Herald acts as a kind of chorus, ushering the audience through the play. So there will be no surprises, he announces what is going to happen: Corday will murder Marat; she will have to come to his door three times before she can enter. He frequently interrupts, using coarsely comic language to describe what is happening in the play. He interjects himself into scenes and at times prompts characters on their lines or actions.

Jean-Paul Marat

Marat is a physician and journalist who played a significant role in the French Revolution. As a character in Sade's inner play—which takes place several years after the war—he is a confused man tortured by his memories and the realization that the revolution did not accomplish what he intended. He is plagued by a skin disease and can only find relief by soaking in a bath, which is where he spends his time on stage.

Marat struggles to organize his thoughts, speaking of his ideals for social reform. It is these ideas he defends as he debates with Sade. "I am the Revolution, "he claims at one point. He criticizes the ruling class, those who survived the revolution and live to again profit from it, and the church, which has contributed to oppression by convincing the poor that they are blessed. "We invented the Revolution but we don't know how to run it," he says. Sade scolds Marat for hiding behind his words and failing to take action; Marat explains that he never believed the pen alone could destroy institutions. He contends that social injustice demands action and that human beings are called to challenge the status quo and change it.

Marat lacks Sade's eloquence, but he seems to truly believe the ideals of which he speaks. When he writes he does so with action in mind, he says, although he is clearly doing nothing more than sitting in his bathtub. By the play's end he is exhausted and filled with doubt about his words and the revolution they helped inspire. He desperately tries to dictate a call to the people of France when he is stabbed by Corday.

Nurses

These are Coulmier's stooges, who keep the patients in line as needed, and overcome Roux when his speeches become too incendiary. They are brutish men who carry batons to beat down the patients.

Patients

These are the insane who populate the play, lurking in the background. They chant to Marat that they want a revolution "NOW!" As the play concludes, they are incited by Sade and Roux and begin rioting, chanting "Revolution! Copulation!" They are savagely beaten by the Nurses.

Jacques Roux

A former priest, Roux levels strong accusations against the church and interjects his radical ideas during Sade's play; at one point he calls for the churches to be closed and turned into schools. His questions and allegations disturb Coulmier and incite the patients. Although he is in a sort of straightjacket and has limited mobility, his mouth is often running. He is frequently pulled to the side by the asylum attendants to be silenced.

Sade

Sade is the author of the inner play. Interred in the Charenton Asylum, he writes plays for the patients to perform. Sixty-eight-years-old, he is fat and noticeably eccentric. He interacts at times with the characters within the play he is directing. He regularly confronts his lead character, Marat, eloquently debating the French Revolution. He exhibits a fascination with death, especially the painful, tortured variety. He admits to a confusion about his role in his ongoing conversation with Marat, saying, "I do not know if I am hangman or victim."

Sade doesn't believe in idealists, only in himself. He describes his imprisonment in the Bastille in which he confronted the criminal within himself, a criminal that committed desecrations and tortures, acts for which he was whipped. Thirteen years of imprisonment have taught him the depths of his own depravity and allowed him to focus his attention on the body—particularly the concept of sadomasochistic sex. Sade's efforts are heroically honest, wrote Penelope Gilliatt in *Vogue*, "but he is neither an admirable nor an enviable man, being without charity and mad."

Marquis de Sade

See Sade

Sisters

These are athletic looking men who are dressed in light grey. They carry rosaries and attend to Corday.

Class Conflict

In this retelling of the French Revolution's aftermath, Weiss raises questions about the struggle between classes, between the aristocracy or privileged class, and the poor, lower class. The picture that he paints is a grim one. The much-needed, much-touted Revolution in France has come. Heads have rolled—literally—and changes in France's government have been introduced. But the question is raised, have things really changed or have the new ruling class adopted the ways of the old aristocracy? The play notes the actions of the ruling class and how the poor are treated. The situation has slightly improved but not enough to merit the loss of life in the revolution.

The church is scrutinized for aiding the ruling class by encouraging those in poverty to turn to God and see merit in suffering. Churches should be made into schools, the play suggests, at least they might then make some positive contribution to society. The lives of the new ruling class are examined, pointing out a basic pattern. Once in power, those who may have started out with good intentions become corrupt. Power corrupts, greed corrupts. The wealth resides with the minority who control society; the pattern is repeated with the rich getting richer, the poor getting poorer.

These messages are couched in the surreal setting of an insane asylum with three major factions (represented by Marat, Sade, and Coulmier) debating the reality of the times and the issues.

Topics for Further Study

- Research the French Revolution of the eighteenth century and the civil rights and antiwar movements in the U.S. in the 1960s. Discuss the similarities and differences in these events and the two time periods.

- Were Sade and Marat insane? Why or why not?

- Research how the Nazis treated artists in the 1930s and 1940s. How may this have influenced Weiss's work?

- Look at the characters of Sade,

Marat, and Coulmier. Name three contemporary characters, real or fictional, that seem most similar to them and illustrate how they are alike.

While this occurs, the insane inmates become agitated and threaten the security of the institution. Coulmier, representing the status quo and those in power, continually defends the present, pointing out the improvements; he is the one most threatened by the unruliness of the patients, who represent the poor masses. Weiss uses the similarities between the oppressed poor and the incarcerated patients to show that inequity existed not only in the French Revolution but in all social situations—even ones as microcosmic as the power structure of an insane asylum.

Weiss held many communist sympathies, and he employs socialist ideology to the events he depicts. He illustrates the theory that oppressed people will rise up to better their conditions in life. In the play within the play, the actors/patients praise Marat's efforts in the revolution, yet they also criticize him for not going far enough. They want continued revolt to the point that real change takes place. While these exhortations seem directed at Marat and the circumstances following the revolution, they can just as easily be applied beyond the setting of Sade's play. Criticism is also leveled at the ruling class of the French society that is represented by the audience members visiting the asylum. More succinctly, the patients' calls for change can be focused on the asylum director, whose efforts at progressive therapy are appreciated but who could also do much more to make life in the asylum better.

Body vs. Mind

Yet the major conflict of *Marat/Sade* is not found between the patients and Coulmier. It lies in the contrasting ideas of Sade and Marat. Sade, as the author of the play within the play, gets to confront Marat and his ideology. Their division is the conflict between the physical world and the mind—or inner world.

Marat represents a deep faith in ideas and ideals. He is tortured at times with the ineffectiveness of words but nonetheless defends their power. Words are a representation of ideas. But he insists he has not fallen back on verbiage to avoid action. Clearly the masses are swayed by words but the sympathies of the crowd are fickle; Marat and his ideas can be rejected. While his concepts were inspiring, Marat's theories of revolution did not go far enough to address the potential for history repeating itself; they have not wrought the revolution that was desired. "We want the revolution NOW," demand the patients. The impoverished and disenfranchised demand that Marat get out of his head and bring change through action. Is the pen mightier than the sword? The play presents the pen as basically impotent. Marat's revolution yields a society too similar to the one he sought to vanquish.

Sade argues with Marat about the ineffectiveness of his thoughts and words. He points out the failure of the revolution to bring real change. Sade believes that the revolution failed because its architects failed to address human nature. He tell Marat that change in society cannot be wrought without first changing man's nature, starting with the body and working outward. To this end Sade proposes his theory of pleasure gained through a combination of agony and ecstasy. By pushing the body to its threshold, one will gain complete knowledge of oneself. Only at that point can humankind hope to change the way they interact.

Appearance vs. Reality

Throughout the play, the traditional barriers between the stage and the audience are broken down. Several times during the course of Sade's play, Coulmier interrupts the action to criticize the work's content. Sade also invades the play's action with his own comments, taking the opportunity to engage Marat in debates on mind and body. Perhaps most unsettling and surreal for the actual viewer (as opposed to the onstage audience represented by Coulmier and his family) are the performances of the inmates enacting the various roles in Sade's drama. It is never clear if their actions are dictated by the Marquis's script and direction or by their own, insane motivations. Similarly, the actors' call for revolution is ambiguous. Weiss does not clarify if the call is directed toward the action in Sade's play, toward Coulmier and his class, or to the actual audience. Many have theorized that it is unimportant who the target is as long as the message is understood.

Style

Play within a Play

Weiss uses the technique of a play within a play to tell his story. This layers the play and creates a certain distance for the audience while providing the playwright with narration to explain the work. Marat is both a character in the inner play and is pulled to the outer play in debates with Sade. Coulmier exists in the outer play and regularly challenges what Sade, the creator of the inner play, is doing.

This technique had been used fairly extensively prior to *Marat/Sade*—notably in the Rodgers and Hammerstein musical *The King and I*. As with Weiss's play, the inner play in *The King and I* addresses issues that are being discussed in the outer play. The slave girl Tuptim acts out *Uncle Tom's Cabin*, a story that she uses as a thinly disguised critique of the King of Siam, for whom the inner play is being performed, and his policy toward his servants. Plays like *The King and I* used the play within play technique for a small section of the overall play. *Marat/Sade*, however, builds its entire foundation on this conceit.

While some critics complained that Weiss's multiple layers were little more than theatrical gimmickry, the majority felt that it was an effective technique that, while failing to answer all questions raised by the plot, made the play a riveting, thought-provoking experience.

Theatre of Cruelty

Weiss was a proponent of a form of experimental theatre known as the Theatre of Cruelty. This was developed primarily by Antonin Artaud, a French actor and director. Artaud wanted theatre to go far beyond the written script (just as Sade wants life to be beyond thoughts and ideas), so elements such as lighting, sound effects, and other forms of technology do not just flesh out the text but play an active role in its presentation and interpretation. In *Marat/Sade* this is employed through the extensive use of special effects such as the gruesome execution sequence.

Albert Bermel wrote in *Artaud's Theatre of Cruelty* that Artaud "did not care whether his characters won or lost arguments. He wanted to use them in order to expose his audiences to a range of their own feelings that was unconscious and therefore normally inaccessible to them." This is evident in the central conflict between Sade and Marat. While Sade's criticism of Marat leads the audience to believe he will offer a solution that Marat's ideas and thoughts could not, they are confounded in this expectation when Sade offers up the concept of carnality. His alternative does little to solve the problems created by the revolution, but it does offer a glimpse into his psyche. In this sense Weiss provokes the audience to consider the character with whom they most identify and which personality traits are closest to their own.

The concept of cruelty for Artaud was the idea of exposing the audience to danger but then to ultimately free them from it, creating a sort of cleansing transformation. Cruelty, as he was using the idea, did not mean actual physical assault but that the energy of the production made as a sort of attack on the defenses of the viewer; it threatened their concept of normality, exposing them to the fragile nature of human interaction. Theatre of Cruelty seeks to make its audience aware that the balance can topple at any moment and everything can be thrown into utter chaos.

In *Marat/Sade* Weiss employs these ideas by creating an environment that is unruly and unsafe. While he allows the actual audience a degree of distance and safety—putting the audience of the inner play at the greatest physical risk—they will nevertheless identify with the inner audience and empathize with their fearful situation. The inmates are odd, ugly, obviously insane. They seem ready to spill over into riot at any moment.

Weiss creates unease with a number of techniques meant to disturb. The play is written in verse form and has song and dance laced throughout it. The Corday character delivers her lines with a sing-song effect, seeming to sleepwalk through her part. This gives her a ghostlike persona that contributes to the surreal effect of watching a play within a play. Added to this is the increasing unrest of the patients, their songs and screams, their threatening behavior. The sum effect of these elements is to unnerve the audience, place them off-balance so that they do not know what to expect. Through this Weiss hoped to confront the audience, make them think, by vicariously putting them through a hellish process he sought to provoke feelings that would not dissipate when the houselights came up.

By many accounts, the impact is significant. The audience may not like it, but they do not forget the experience. As director Brook said of his staging in the introduction to the published version of *Marat/Sade,* 'I know of one acid test in the theatre. It is literally an acid test. When a performance is over, what remains? Fun can be forgotten, but powerful emotion also disappears and good arguments lose their thread. When emotion and argument are harnessed to a wish from the audience to see more clearly into itself—then something in the mind burns. The event scorches onto the memory an outline, a taste, a trace, a smell—a picture. It is the play's central image that remains, its silhouette, and if the elements are rightly blended this silhouette will be its meaning, this shape will be the essence of what it has to say."

Brechtian Influence

Weiss readily admitted his debt to Bertolt Brecht, a German dramatist who lived from 1898-1956. Brecht was known for an approach to epic theatre which he used to make social criticism while using a technique called "Alienation." Brook explained this concept in the introduction to *Marat/Sade:* "Alienation is the art of placing an action at a distance so that it can be judged objectively and so that it can be seen in relation to the world—or rather worlds—around it."

Historical Context

The History of the Play within the Play

It's important to understand the historical events chronicled in *Marat/Sade*. Although part of Sade's drama is fiction it is based on actual events. Jean-Paul Marat was murdered by Charlotte Corday in 1793. He was a physician and journalist who used his newspaper as a platform for his political beliefs.

As a member of the Jacobin party, he played an instrumental part in instigating the French Revolution. The Marquis de Sade was an author living in France during the time of the revolution. He had been imprisoned for his cruel sexual practices (the term "sadism" is a derivation of his name and is used to describe sexual pleasure gained through the causing of pain). He was in residence at the Asylum at Charenton and did write plays while there. He did not know Marat but did give a memorial address at his funeral.

The French Revolution actually took place between 1787 and 1799, with a major climax in 1789, when an outraged mob stormed the Bastille, a fortress and prison. Later the French royal family was forced to flee and the king, Louis XVI, was captured and executed. Leadership in the government thereafter brought about a Reign of Terror in which perceived enemies of the cause were sought out and slaughtered. Later, Napoleon Bonaparte assumed power and built France into a considerable empire. Reasons for the revolution are many, the strongest being the impoverished state of the peasants and the lack of any political power by the middle class. *Marat/Sade* is set in 1808, when the Revolution was over, but the play reenacts an important event from those bloody days—the assassination of Marat, one of the revolutions' key architects.

The Foundation of Weiss's Politics

Weiss experienced three major wars in his lifetime. World War I was in full swing when he was born, the second World War sent his family into exile, and, at the time he was writing *Marat/Sade*, the Vietnam War was escalating into a vicious battle of attrition. Having experienced the cruel effects of dictatorship firsthand, Weiss came to oppose fascist governments of any kind. He found a positive alternative to such oppressive rule in the concepts of communism, which idealizes equality of ownership and government by the people.

At the time he was developing the play, former Nazi leaders were being tried for war crimes committed during World War II. In the United States, the year 1964 was pivotal because it marked the Tonkin Bay incident in Vietnam and the official authorization by Congress to involve U.S. troops in that conflict. The country was recovering from the assassination the year before of President John F. Kennedy.

This timeframe was also the beginning of other significant action in the U.S., most notably the start of the civil rights movement as well as the women's movement. The civil rights movement was marked by violence and race riots in major cities. The energy of the movement gathered steam and rolled over into the antiwar movement. The 1960s were revolutionary times with a preponderance of both peaceful and violent demonstrations against the government.

Compare & Contrast

- **1787:** Responding to increasing economic pressures caused by war, poor harvest, inequitable taxation, and the extravagances of the monarchy, Louis the XVI of France convenes the Estates General. Although this seems a victory for the aristocracy, it is really the beginning of the revolution.

  1964: Following the directions put in place by the late President Kennedy, President Lyndon Johnson calls for victory in the "war on poverty" and signs into law The Economic Opportunity Act, creating an Officer of Economic Opportunity. This office was to oversee a myriad of agencies providing services to the poor, ensuring better nutrition, health, and education for the underprivileged.

Today: Conservative leadership has eroded funding for government programs aiding the poor. Welfare and programs for health and education to inner cities have been severely curtailed or completely phased out. The disparity between the poor and the wealthy grows.

- **1793:** The French Revolution begins, as the poor rise up to overthrow the monarchy in one of the bloodiest wars of the eighteenth century.

  1964: North Vietnamese fire at a U.S. destroyer in the Tonkin Gulf, off the coast of Vietnam. The Tonkin Gulf Resolution is passed giving the President authority to take military action; this essentially launches the Vietnam War, in which U.S. forces fight in South Vietnam, opposing the communist threat from North Vietnam.

  Today: The Communist Party has dissipated with the dissolution of the Soviet Union and Eastern European countries. East and West Germany are reunited. The U.S. continues to wage small military actions, mostly in the Middle East, but where Vietnam was long and bloody, current wars rely on technology and have resulted in minimal loss of American life.

- **1789:** The National Assembly of France introduces the "Declaration of the Rights of Man and the Citizen."
1964: The Civil Rights Bill is passed after a lengthy and bitter fight by southern senators. The bodies of three civil rights workers are discovered in Mississippi, the victim of white supremacists. Race riots erupt in Harlem and Philadelphia. Atlanta restaurant owner Lester Maddox closes his restaurant rather than be forced to serve blacks. His stance against integration leads him to the governorship of Georgia. Civil rights leader Martin Luther King, Jr. is awarded the Nobel Peace Prize.
Today: Although schools and neighborhoods have been integrated, racism has not been eliminated. The conservative agenda includes elimination of affirmative action measures which insure fair and even preferential treatment for minorities. Neo-Nazis and other white

supremist groups are on the rise. African Americans have attained positions of power, including seats in the U.S. senate and House of Representatives and Supreme Court appointments.

But like Weiss's play (Marat's concepts), much of the rhetoric of the 1960s was merely that, and although important issues were addressed, things didn't necessarily change. Or not that much. Those in power within the resistance movement, mostly white males, were reticent to accept women as much other than sex objects. So those who were disenfranchised continued in that state. Gains were made in civil rights but it has become apparent in the decades following that racism cannot be legislated away. These events were hard to ignore and many have speculated that they in some way influenced the themes of *Marat/Sade*.

The Culture of 1960s

In literature, the 1950s produced a generation of beatniks, bohemian artists who lived on the edge of society and actively criticized the government and society. This movement spread and spawned the hippies of the 1960s. One notable poet of the Beat Generation, as it was called, was Allen Ginsberg, whose long diatribes against America were laced with profanity and references to sex and drugs. His *Howl*, which was first published in 1956, started out with this line: "I saw the best minds of my generation destroyed by madness. . . ." Another poem titled *America* starts with this: "America I've given you all and now I'm nothing/America two dollars and twenty-seven cents January 17, 1956/I can't stand my own mind/America when will we end the human war?"

Artists during this time included Andy Warhol who was shocking and questioning artistic values with his silk screens of pop icons done larger than life, including the Campbell soup can and Marilyn Monroe. The Beatles made their first trip to the U.S. in 1964, wedging a chasm between generations of music lovers. The folk music of Bob Dylan and Joan Baez was popular, inspiring musicians to address political and social issues in their compositions. Folk music—and later rock—became a foundation from which to protest such topics as the war and racism.

Critical Overview

When the work *Marat/Sade* was first produced, it became a bit of a joke to some. A common jibe was often directed at the play's lengthy name: "No, I haven't seen the play, but I've read the title." The first production of the play was staged in West Berlin, Germany, under the direction of Konrad Swinarski. From the start the work was controversial, which is often the best publicity. In its initial run, many critics saw the influence of fellow German Bertolt Brecht on Weiss and his play. Weiss admitted his debt to the great playwright, stating "Brecht influenced me as a dramatist. I learnt most from Brecht. I learnt clarity from him, the necessity of making clear the social question in a play. I learnt from his lightness. He is never heavy in the psychological German way." Of this first production, the London *Times* claimed it was "the most ambitious example of the Theatre of Cruelty yet to appear. Practically every influence current in operation in intellectual high fashion is to be found in this play."

It was the direction of Peter Brook and his London production of the play, however, that brought *Marat/Sade* to the highest level of international critical acclaim. Brook attended rehearsals for the first production in West Berlin and there met Weiss. The two agreed to take the play to London, where Brook would reinterpret it and later move the production to New York. The

Brook-directed version made its debut at the Aldwych Theatre in 1964.

As with the German production, the London performances almost immediately sparked controversy, including a verbal attack on the play by a member of the theatre company's executive council. Critics also had a good deal to say about Weiss's work. Millie Painter-Downes of the *New Yorker* called it "a dazzling theatrical experience" and a "stunning production." She ended her favorable review by stating, "It is an electrifying show, which would have been a hit even without the present controversy."

While most reviewers conceded the work's originality, their appraisals were mixed. A critic from *Newsweek* questioned whether Weiss should be considered a revolutionary playwright: "Beneath all the business, all the violence and startling gestures, is a vacuum. Weiss, for all his pretensions, is a conventional socialist and an extremely limited philosopher." The critic went on to say that although the play is impressive, "it establishes a kind of frenetic dance, a choreographed quest for the truths of the imagination, flattering our sense of the fashionable, our desire to be at wicked, important happenings, but offering no light and no resurrection, *Marat/Sade* is to be seen but not believed." A reviewer for *Time* labeled it "inspired sensationalism, "while Harold Clurman of the *Nation* called it "fascinating entertainment." Clurman both praised and questioned the work, seeing it as a dialogue with the spirit of the playwright yet he also appraised that the text, when removed from Brook's theatrics, was trite.

One of the most disturbing parts of the Brook production followed the play's proper ending. At the curtain call, the actors would clap back to the audience in a rhythmic pattern which had the effect of shutting up the audience, "dismissing us scornfully as representatives of a public that has evaded its responsibility to recognize the horrendous atrocity of life within us and around us," claimed Henry Hewes in the *Saturday Review*.

While such gestures were startling and unconventional—and many critics found them patently offensive—few could deny the power of such theatrics. While a critical consensus could not be reached regarding the artistic merits of *Marat/Sade*, most agreed that it is a singular work deserving attention. Thirty years after its initial production, Weiss's play is still considered innovative and shocking; it is regarded as a hallmark of progressive theatre.

What Do I Read Next?

- *Mother Courage and Her Children* (1939) is a well-known and often performed play by Bertolt Brecht. The play is set during the Thirty Years War and is considered a masterpiece.

- Herman Hesse's *Beneath the Wheel* (1906) is a good example of the work of this writer who was a friend and mentor to Weiss. This book looks at the duality of man through a story of two students.

- Martin Esslin wrote a small book titled *Antonin Artaud* (1976). This work offers a quick look at Artaud's ideas about the Theatre of Cruelty.

- Howard Barker's *Scenes from an Execution* (1984) deals with an historical event and is produced in an experimental fashion.

- Written in 1951, *Saint Joan* by George Bernard Shaw looks at the life and ultimate execution of Joan of Arc. Like Weiss's drama, Shaw's work is very political.

- Janet Frame's *Faces in the Water* (1961) is a novel that examines the mentally ill residing in institutions.

- Another German writer who influenced Weiss was Franz Kafka. *Complete Stories and Parables* (1946) is a good introduction to this important writer.

Sources

Bermel, Albert. *Artaud 's Theatre of Cruelty*, Tallinger, 1977.

Brook, Peter. *The Empty Space*, Avon, 1968.

Brook, Peter. Introduction to *Marat/Sade*, by Peter Weiss, Atheneum, 1965.

Clurman, Harold. Review of *Marat/Sade* in the *Nation*, January 17, 1966.

Ellis, Roger. *Peter Weiss in Exile: A Critical Study of His Works*, UMI Research Press, 1987.

Gilliatt, Penelope. "Peter Brook: A Natural Saboteur of Order" in *Vogue*, January 1, 1966.

Ginsberg, Allen. *Howl and Other Poems*, City Lights Books, 1956.

Hewes, Henry. Review of *Marat/Sade* in the *Saturday Review*, January 15, 1966.

Hilton, Ian. *Peter Weiss: A Search for Affinities*, Oswald Wolff, 1970.

Jones, David Richard. *Great Directors at Work: Stanislavsky, Brecht, Kazan, Brook*, University of California Press, 1986.

Kushner, Tony. "The Art of the Difficult" in *Civilization*, *August/September*, 1997.

Painter-Downes, Mollie. Review of *Marat/Sade* in the *New Yorker*, September 19, 1964.

Review of *Marat/Sade* in *Newsweek*, January 10, 1966.

Review of *Marat/Sade* in *Time*, January 7, 1966.

Further Reading

Cohen, Robert. *Understanding Peter Weiss*, University of South Carolina Press, 1993.

> This work provides a good biographical overview of Weiss's life as well as a critical study of his work, including a whole section on *Marat/Sade*.

Connor, Clifford D. *Jean Paul Marat: Scientist and Revolutionary*, Humanities Press, 1993.

> This is a biography of Marat, looking at his life both before and after the Revolution.

Schama, Simon. *Citizens: A Chronicle of the French Revolution*, Vintage Books, 1988.

> This book provides some insight into the events and significance of the French Revolution. It offers a useful overview of the events depicted in Sade's play within the play.

Weiss, Peter. *Exile: A Novel*, Delacorte, 1968.

> This is an English translation of two of Weiss's autobiographical novels, *The Leavetaking* and *Vanishing Point*.

www.ingramcontent.com/pod-product-compliance
Ingram Content Group UK Ltd.
Pitfield, Milton Keynes, MK11 3LW, UK
UKHW021951140225
455059UK00010B/225

9 781375 383950